MW01061270

BEHIND A
FROWNING
PROVIDENCE

John J. Murray

Retired Minister of the Edinburgh
Congregation of the Free Church
of Scotland (Continuing)

THE BANNER OF TRUTH TRUST

THE BANNER OF TRUTH TRUST
3 Murrayfield Road, Edinburgh EH12 6EL, UK
PO Box 621, Carlisle, PA 17013, USA

*

© The Banner of Truth Trust 1990
First published 1990
Reprinted 1994
Reprinted 1998
Reprinted 2002
Reprinted 2005
Reprinted 2011
Reprinted 2017

ISBN: 978 0 85151 572 4

*

Typeset in 10.5/13 Adobe Garamond Pro at
The Banner of Truth Trust, Edinburgh

Printed in the USA by
Versa Press, Inc.,
East Peoria, IL

IN MEMORY OF
LYNDA JOAN [1967–80]

Introduction

One of the best known hymns is William Cowper's 'God moves in a mysterious way, His wonders to perform'. Cowper was subject to melancholy and knew more about the darker side of Christian experience than the brighter. It was out of heart-felt experience that he composed his hymn and presented in it so many precious gems of truth such as the oft-quoted lines,

> *Behind a frowning providence*
> *He hides a smiling face.*

What is meant by a 'frowning providence'? Is this something that we are to expect in the Christian life? If so, how do we cope with it?

Like you, I have sought answers to these questions. Some of them I hope to share in the following pages.

1: There is a Providence

Providence is an old-fashioned word and has a strange ring to modern ears. Yet when we break it down into its parts the meaning becomes clear. It comes from the Latin *video* 'to see' and *pro* 'before', meaning 'to see beforehand'. In our lives we plan beforehand but we do not see what is going to happen. God has planned everything for his creation and because he is the sovereign God everything will come to pass as he purposed. Providence is that marvellous working of God by which all the events and happenings in his universe accomplish the purpose he has in mind.

The scriptural doctrine that God 'works all things according to the counsel of his will' is clearly set out in the Westminster Confession of Faith's definition of God's Eternal Decree:

> God from all eternity did, by the most wise and holy counsel of his own will, freely and unchangeably ordain whatsoever comes to pass: yet so, as thereby neither is God the author of sin, nor is violence offered to the will of the creatures, nor is the liberty or contingency of second causes taken away, but rather established (*Chap.* III, 1).

The Shorter Catechism asks the question: 'How does God execute his decrees?' and answers 'God executes his decrees in the works of creation and providence' (Q. 8). What about redemption? It is included in the work of providence! It is the supreme work of providence.

In it God sent his Son into this world for the purpose of redeeming a people. He set his love on hell-deserving sinners and chose them in Christ before the foundation of the world. Those he foreknew he predestined that they might be 'conformed to the image of his Son' (*Rom.* 8:29). God has a plan for his church that stretches from eternity to eternity.

In relation to that grand purpose, 'God has', according to Thomas Boston, 'by an eternal decree, immovable as mountains of brass (*Zech.* 6:1), appointed the whole of everyone's lot, the crooked parts thereof, as well as the straight.' As Job said in the midst of his sufferings: 'He performeth the thing that is appointed for me' (*Job* 23:14).

The plan of God extends to every detail in my life. There are several important things that can be said of it:

1. *The plan is perfect.* Everything that God does is perfect. It may not appear to me at times to be perfect but it is, because it will ultimately lead to the greater glory of God.

2. *The plan is exhaustive.* It includes everything. It is worked out in a situation where everything is under the control of God. It extends to the smallest and most casual things. 'The very hairs of your head are all numbered' (*Matt.* 10:30).

3. *The plan is for my ultimate good.* Everyone who loves God has the assurance that 'all things work together for good' (*Rom.* 8:28). If God is for me who can be against me? The opposition does not count. The gracious purpose of God will certainly be accomplished in my life.

4. *The plan is secret.* God alone knows what is going to happen in advance because he has purposed it all. Every detail is fixed before I was born. God hides it from me until it happens. I discover it day by day as the plan unfolds. This is the unfolding of his secret will for my life.

Although God has only one will we often speak about his secret will and his revealed will. The latter is made known in the Scriptures and is the rule of our duty. The former is made known in his providence and is to be submitted to and observed.

This teaching is clearly set out in the words of Thomas Boston:

> Whoever would walk with God must be due observers of the Word and Providence of God for by these in a special manner he manifests himself to his people. In the one we see what he says; in the other what he does. These are the two books that every student of holiness ought to be much conversant in. They are both written with the one hand and they should both be carefully read by those who would have not only the name of religion but the thing. They should be studied together if we would profit by either for being taken together they give light one to the other; and as it is our duty to read the Word, so also it is our duty to observe the work of God.

These words are taken from a sermon on Psalm 107:43: 'Whoso is wise and will observe these things, even they shall understand the lovingkindness of the LORD'. If we are to fulfil the duty of observing 'these things' the qualification required is wisdom but the benefit is that we will understand the lovingkindness of the Lord. We know how a human being stands related to us by his or her behaviour. If we study God's behaviour towards his children we will see his love. Providence has its own language.

We need to observe the different kinds of providences. There are uncommon providences, such as miracles, and there are what might be called common providences, like the refreshing rain. There are great providences, like the crossing of the Red Sea and there are what seem small providences, like a king not being able to sleep at night. There are favourable or smiling providences and there are what appear to be dark, cross or frowning providences.

If, as we believe, a frowning providence comes from the hand of the same Father as a smiling providence how can we reconcile these things? How can we justify the ways of God with us?

2: There are Dark Providences

It is the presence of the dark providences in the universe and in our lives that go a long way to make up what John Flavel called 'the mystery of providence'. Thomas Boston addressed himself to the same problem in a series of sermons on Ecclesiastes 7: 13: 'Consider the work of God: for who can make that straight which he hath made crooked'. They were published after his death under the title *The Crook in the Lot*.

When adversity comes into our lives we tend to react in one of two ways. We may say that it is from a source other than God and he has no power to stop it; or we may say it is an evidence of God's anger against us. Either way we are guilty of casting aspersions on the character of our Father and consequently of perverting our attitude to him. 'A just (right) view of afflicting incidents', says Boston in the opening sentence of his work, 'is altogether necessary to a Christian deportment under them'. He continues: 'That view is to be obtained only by faith, not by sense; for it is the light of the Word alone that represents them justly, discerning in them the work of God, and consequently designs becoming the divine perfections.'

The Christian, although he is justified, remains a sinner in the midst of a fallen world. He is subject to 'all the ills that flesh is heir to'. Some of the consequences of his past sins affect his life. He is subject to the discipline of his heavenly Father. Satan concentrates his attack on him. The world under the control of the evil one is hostile to him. His sufferings are compounded because he is a Christian. 'In the world', our Lord warned his disciples, 'you will have tribulation' (*John* 16:33).

The Bible leaves us in no doubt that suffering is a normal part of the true Christian life. Hebrews chapter 11 portrays the suffering witnesses of the Old Testament. The New Testament presents us with our great Example who was 'made perfect through sufferings' (*Heb.* 2:10), and also with the many followers who became 'partakers' in his sufferings (*1 Pet.* 4:13). The whole emphasis in the teaching of the early church was on 'rejoicing in the midst of sufferings.' It is 'through much tribulation' that we enter the kingdom (*Acts* 14:22).

The Westminster Confession of Faith contains in its chapter on Providence this judiciously-worded paragraph on God's dealings with his own children:

> The most wise, righteous and gracious God, doth oftentimes leave for a season his own children to manifold temptations, and the corruption of their own hearts, to chastise them for their former sins, or to discover unto them the hidden strength of corruption and deceitfulness of their own hearts, that they may be humbled; and to raise them to a more close and constant dependence for their support upon himself, and to make them more watchful against all future occasions of sin, and for sundry other just and holy ends.

Sadly such teaching seems far removed from the outlook that prevails in large parts of the church today. The impression is given that the purpose of the Christian life is enjoyment. Everything that stands in the way of that is to be eliminated. People are looking for a problem-free Christianity. The health, wealth and success gospel is having a field day. Purveyors of such a gospel look the part. Unfortunately, the hollowness of such views becomes apparent when suffering, sorrow or disappointment comes. Then it becomes clear that we need a faith that is grounded in God's Word.

3: God's Designs in Dark Providences

Having seen that trials or dark providences are part of the Christian way we must now inquire into their purpose. While it is always wrong to react in rebellion and anger against God's dealings with us, it is right to consider why they are part of our lot. There is a right and a wrong way of asking 'Why?' We must reflect on what God is doing. What is the Lord seeking to teach us through these unpleasant experiences? Here are some of the designs that God has in our sufferings:

1. Sufferings are to try us

'The crook in the lot', says Boston, 'is the great engine of providence for making men appear in their true colours'. C. S. Lewis once referred to sufferings as 'blockades on the road to hell'. The same sun that melts the ice also hardens the clay. Says Andrew Fuller, 'Afflictions refine some, they consume others'. The test of a person's Christianity is what happens in the storm, when the house is battered in the winds of affliction.

The faith of the Christian is tried and tested, wrote Simon Peter (*1 Pet.* 1:3–7). It is the trial that determines the authenticity of our faith. Peter reminds the Christians to whom he writes of the great hope they have, although for the present they are grieved by the many trials. The reason for this is that God is sitting as a refiner of gold. He wants to bring out the pure gold of naked trust in himself. When all the dross of self-trust is purged out then faith will be to the praise, honour and glory of Jesus Christ.

Abraham was a man of faith and he endured the trial of faith. God commanded him to leave his comfortable life in Ur and go out on the strength of a promise that he would give him a land and a seed. But the promise never seemed to be fulfilled. There was no sign of an heir. In the impatience of unbelief Abraham tried to do it his way. Hagar's son Ishmael was the result, but God will have none of it. Ishmael must go. Another eleven years later and the son of promise is born. But Isaac must be laid on the altar. Until God had Isaac he did not have all of Abraham that there was. God speaks as if he had newly discovered the faith of Abraham: 'Now I know that you fear God' (*Gen.* 22:12). Abraham had come through the test. His faith was pure gold.

> *When through fiery trials thy pathway shall lie,*
> *My grace all-sufficient shall be thy supply;*
> *The flame shall not hurt thee; I only design*
> *Thy dross to consume, and thy gold to refine.*

2. Sufferings are to expose our sins

When we set off on the Christian pathway we do not know much about our true selves. It is even possible to enter the Christian ministry without much knowledge of the deceitfulness of the heart. 'We are on too good terms with ourselves', said Dr Lloyd-Jones. 'We don't know much about dust and ashes'. We pray sincerely for growth in grace, for increase in faith, but the answer comes in a way we did not expect. John Newton was one who made the painful discovery:

> *I asked the Lord that I might grow*
> *In faith and love and every grace,*
> *Might more of his salvation know,*
> *And seek more earnestly his face.*
>
> *'Twas he who taught me thus to pray;*
> *And he, I trust, has answered prayer;*
> *But it has been in such a way*
> *As almost drove me to despair.*

I hoped that, in some favoured hour,
At once he'd answer my request,
And by his love's constraining power
Subdue my sins, and give me rest.

Instead of this, he made me feel
The hidden evils of my heart,
And let the angry powers of hell
Assault my soul in every part.

Robert Murray M'Cheyne confessed that the seed of every known sin was to be found in his heart. What latent corruption there is within! We are like a petro-chemical plant. It takes only a spark to set us alight. Think of the break-out of sin in the lives of so many of the saints —Abraham with his deceit; Job with his rash words; Moses with his anger; Asaph with his murmuring; Paul with his pride. Job could say, 'I abhor myself and repent in dust and ashes' (*Job* 42:6). Asaph had to say, 'I was foolish and ignorant; I was as a beast before thee' (*Psa.* 73:22).

Such discoveries make us think less of ourselves and therefore lead us to think more of the Lord Jesus Christ. They bring new depths of repentance and a recovery of a true sense of our own sinfulness.

3. Sufferings are to build character

Whatever else we may have, if we do not have character we have nothing. It is character that determines destiny. The only failure that matters in the end is the failure to build character. In ordinary life character is formed by overcoming difficulties. The state of our society today militates against character building. Even in the church young people are not exposed to the influences that will build character. No wonder so many remain spiritual babes.

We see a renowned athlete winning a gold medal. He may make it look easy on the day, but victory could not have been achieved without painstaking training and meeting increasingly tough opposition. The process by which God builds character is outlined in Romans 5:1-5. Paul says that 'We glory in tribulations'. The Greek word translated 'tribulation' comes from the verb 'to press'. The word is used to describe the crushing of the grapes and olives. The figure suggests the heavy pressures of outward trouble or inward anguish. Tribulation produces 'patient endurance'—the ability to stay with it and not fall apart. This brave endurance in turn produces what the Authorized (King James) Version translates as experience but which is more accurately translated as 'character'—the character which results from a process of trial.

We might be tempted to ask whether God can build character without suffering. That is a hypothetical question. He has not chosen to do so. Young Joseph gave every indication that he was spoiled. He was not fit to be a leader. It took the pit and the prison and twenty-two years of preparation before he was ready to do the work God intended him to do. In the prison he was laid in irons (*Psa.* 105:18). Variant readings are 'the iron entered into his soul' and 'his soul entered into iron'. It was more than Joseph's flesh that felt the iron.

God prepares us as if there were no one else to prepare. A sculptor working at a piece of marble when asked: 'What are you doing?' replied, 'I am chipping away everything that does not look like a horse' .

4. Sufferings bring us to know God better

Sufferings teach us lessons that we cannot learn in College. We may have been to College or Seminary and have a string of letters after our name; we may have read all the great classics in theology and be able to argue on the finer points of divinity; and yet our knowledge may be largely theoretical. It is one thing to know about God; it is another thing to know God. The essence of eternal life is 'that they may know thee the only true God' (*John* 17:3). Paul's ambition was 'that I may know him' (*Phil.* 3:10).

Many Christians can testify that they have learned more about God in the furnace of affliction than in all their previous experiences. Job is a classic example. The Lord said of him, 'There is none like him on earth, a blameless and upright man, one who fears God and shuns evil' (*Job* 1:8), so God put on display one of the trophies of his grace. Satan is given leave to afflict Job. The real question is: What kind of a person is Job? Does he fear God for nothing? (*Job* 1:9). Is his religion only one of self-interest? Ignorant of the battle going on in the heavenly realms Job has many questions to ask. The interesting thing is that he does not get specific answers. What he gets is a revelation of God which at length brings him to confess, 'I have heard of thee by the hearing of the ear but now my eye sees thee. Therefore I abhor myself and repent in dust and ashes' (*Job* 42:5-6).

There are areas of the Word of God that we cannot comprehend until we have experienced suffering. For thirty years of my Christian life I neither understood nor was particularly drawn to the book of Job. Along with a particular time of suffering came the help to understanding it. Martin Luther had a similar testimony: 'Affliction is the Christian's theologian'; 'I never knew the meaning of God's Word until I came into affliction'; 'My temptations have been my masters in divinity'; 'No man, without trials and temptations, can attain a true understanding of the Holy Scriptures'.

> *I walked a mile with pleasure,*
> *She chatted all the way,*
> *But left me none the wiser*
> *For all she had to say.*
>
> *I walked a mile with sorrow*
> *And ne'er a word said she,*
> *But oh the things I learned from her,*
> *When sorrow walked with me.*

5. Sufferings produce fruit in our lives and prepare us for usefulness

In John 15 our Lord compares Christians to branches in a vine. He is the vine and his Father is the vinedresser. The Father looks for fruit from the branches in the vine. Such fruit is dependent on union with Christ but its quality is also related to the Father's pruning. Sometimes the pruning can be drastic. The cutting knife can be sharp. But the whole purpose is spiritual fruit for the glory of God.

No doubt there will be many humble believers in glory whose names were hardly known on earth but who will be laden with fruit. Perhaps they carried such sorrows in this world that they could not share with others and persevered at God's throne of grace where they became mighty warriors for the kingdom. Said Phillips Brooks, 'Wherever souls are being tried and ripened in whatever commonplace and homely way there God is hewing out the pillars of his temple'. Thomas Boston reminds us, 'There is never an act of resignation to the will of God under the cross, nor an act of trust in him for his help, but they will be recorded in heaven's register as good works.'

Sufferings can bring a new dimension of fruitfulness into our lives. They can produce a new gentleness and a tenderness. This was evident in the life of Dr Martyn Lloyd-Jones and never more so than in his later years. During his own sufferings he remembered others who suffered. In the last year of his life our daughter became seriously ill and died at the age of thirteen. As soon as he heard he wrote us a most comforting letter. Within three months he himself entered glory. Mrs Lloyd-Jones later shared with us the tenderness of his concern: 'I wish you could have heard his prayers for your little daughter's illness and death. He never forgot and had such tender concern for her and for you all in your sorrow and mourning. It is a glorious thing to belong to the family of God. We really feel for each other.'

We often see sorrows leading to increased usefulness in the lives of God's servants. 'God', says Spurgeon, 'gets his best soldiers out of the highlands of affliction'. He was an outstanding example of this himself. He says:

> I do not know whether my experience is that of all God's people; but I am afraid that all the grace I have got at any of my comfortable and easy times and happy hours might almost be on a penny. But the good I have received from my sorrows, and pains and griefs is altogether incalculable.

Thomas Boston who had an abundant share of sorrows remarked, 'It is the usual way of providence with me that blessing comes through several iron gates'. 'The tools the great Architect intends to use much', J. C. Ryle wrote in the same vein, 'are often kept long in the fire to temper them and fit them for the work'.

Examples of this truth abound in Scripture and in church history and are too numerous to mention. We may think of Paul and his painful affliction, 'a thorn in the flesh', and the purpose for which it was sent: 'Most gladly will I glory in my infirmities that the power of Christ may rest on me' (*2 Cor.* 12:7-9). We may think of Rutherford banished to the cold—physical and spiritual—of Aberdeen where

> . . . *in my sea-beat prison*
> *My Lord and I held tryst.*

From that place of affliction there poured forth the *Letters* full of the fragrance of Christ that have enriched the church down the centuries. We may think of John Bunyan cast into prison for refusing to keep silence, his usefulness seemingly curtailed. But God multiplied his usefulness through his pen in the writing of *Pilgrim's Progress*. Then we have Thomas Boston suffering from poor health, with his children sick and dying, his wife crippled by mental illness, dealing with difficult parishioners, engaged in ecclesiastical wrangles, labouring in relative obscurity; yet out of it all have come writings that have brought untold blessing to multitudes. No wonder John Flavel wrote: 'Oh the blessed chemistry of heaven to extract such mercies out of such miseries!'

6. Sufferings lead us to make God our all and to prepare us for glory

Sufferings drive us to God. We set out in service thinking God needs us. We soon find out that we need him. 'When God lays men on their backs, then they look up to heaven', says Thomas Watson. We cry to God for blessings but we do not really want him. He has to teach us that *he* is the greatest blessing of all.

This was the discovery made by John Newton in his hymn 'Prayer Answered by Crosses', already quoted. He goes on:

> *Yea, more, with his own hand he seemed*
> *Intent to aggravate my woe,*
> *Crossed all the fair designs I schemed,*
> *Blasted my gourds, and laid me low.*
>
> *Lord, why is this? I trembling cried;*
> *Wilt thou pursue this worm to death?*
> *This is the way, the Lord replied,*
> *I answer prayer for grace and faith.*
>
> *These inward trials I now employ*
> *From self and pride to set thee free,*
> *And break thy schemes of earthly joy,*
> *That thou may'st seek thy all in me.*

In Psalm 73 Asaph recounts his experience of nearly falling: 'my steps had nearly slipped' (*Psa.* 73:2). While the wicked were prospering he was being plagued and chastened. He was perplexed and baffled until he went into the sanctuary of God. There he saw things in their true light. The outcome was that he confessed: 'Whom have I in heaven but thee? And there is none upon earth that I desire beside thee' (*Psa.* 73:25). God had become the all-sufficient portion of his soul.

In this way God prepares us for glory. If we lived for nothing but a life of comfort and ease here there would be no desire for the blessedness to come. 'God will have his people sigh and groan on the way to glory,' writes Maurice Roberts. Thomas Watson emphasises the same lesson: 'The vessels of mercy are first seasoned with affliction and then the wine of glory is poured in'.

4: Our Comfort in Dark Providences

1. There is always a purpose of love behind dark providences

One of the most difficult things to do when the road is rough or when the billows are passing over us is to feel that God still loves us. It is the last thing we can accept. But we are not called to feel; we are called to believe. In his book, *In All Their Afflictions*, Murdoch Campbell tells of a minister in the North of Scotland who suddenly lost his spiritually-minded wife. As he prayed that night in the presence of friends he said, 'If an angel from heaven told me that this would work for my good I would not believe him but because thy Word says it I must believe it.'

We are to measure God's love not by his providence but by his promise. 'When we cannot trace God's hand we can trust God's heart', says C. H. Spurgeon. When providences are dark it is difficult to read them. It is the Word that tells us how to view them.

> *Judge not the Lord by feeble sense,*
> *But trust him for his grace;*
> *Behind a frowning providence*
> *He hides a smiling face.*

By faith we have to trace it all to the hand of our Father. The 'crook in the lot' is all of God's making. We are prone to stop at second causes. We may look at doctors who may have been negligent. We may think of drivers who have been careless. We may feel bitterness over 'what might have been'.

Joseph after suffering the greatest indignities at the hand of his brothers traced it all to the hand of God: 'But as for you, you meant evil against me but God meant it for good, in order to bring it about as it is this day, to save people alive' (*Gen.* 50:20). Job suffered at the hands of the Chaldeans and Sabeans yet when he came to speak of his loss he was able to say, 'The Lord gave and the Lord has taken away; blessed be the name of the Lord' (*Job* 1:21). Joseph left his cause in the hand of God and he was vindicated. Job did the same. Says Samuel Rutherford,

> It is impossible to be submissive and religiously patient if you stay your thoughts down among the confused rollings and wheels of second causes, O, the place! O, the time! O, if this had been, this had not followed!

2. There is much that remains a mystery and for which there is no immediate answer

This lies at the very crux of the matter. It may seem a strange paradox but it was when Job was willing not to understand that he began to understand.

> *God moves in a mysterious way*
> *His wonders to perform;*
> *He plants his footsteps in the sea,*
> *And rides upon the storm.*
>
> *Deep in unfathomable mines*
> *Of never-failing skill*
> *He treasures up his bright designs,*
> *And works his sovereign will.*

And why should this not be so? God is God and man is man. It is in keeping with the greatness of God. In a sermon on John 13:7 entitled 'Dark Providences Made Clear in Due Time,' Ralph Erskine explains God's purpose in dark providences thus:

> It is to discover himself in a way suitable to himself and his glorious perfections and to show that his thoughts are not our thoughts nor his ways our ways. If he should work according

to our thoughts and imaginations how would it appear that he is Jehovah, a sovereign God that acts like himself?

God owes us no explanations. We owe him implicit trust and obedience. It is not easy to trust God when he appears to be silent, as he was with Job, but trust we must.

Dr Ronald Dunn has these wise words to say on the problem of the silence of God in suffering:

> I think this is the hardest part of all. You can take just about anything, if you know why. Everywhere I go, every meeting, I'm asked—Why? . . . I'm going to tell you something: God will very seldom answer your question of Why. It is not that there are no answers, it's just that you and I probably wouldn't be able to comprehend the answer if God were to tell us, and besides that, we have to learn to trust him without knowing why. We ask him questions. What we're usually doing is saying, 'Lord explain yourself', calling God into account (*Walking with the King*, p 173).

There appears to be an obsession today with 'Why me?' Books which claim to have an answer to all our problems top the Christian best-sellers lists. One book that enjoyed a wide circulation, especially in the United States, Rabbi Harold Kushner's *When Bad Things Happen to Good People*, gave this answer to the problem of suffering: God is a limited God. 'God would like people to get what they deserve in life but he cannot always arrange it'. A reply to this came from the pen of Warren Wiersbe in his book, *Why Us?* and sub-titled 'When bad things happen to God's people'.

Wiersbe also has some most helpful insights from the sufferings of Job. He writes:

> One of the reasons God did not answer Job's cries for justice was because he wanted to continue his relationship with Job on the basis of grace. God didn't want Job to have 'commercial faith' based on a celestial contract. He wanted Job to have faith in a God with such richness of character—love, mercy,

grace, goodness, kindness—that nothing could interfere with their relationship. Because the key question is not 'Why do the righteous suffer?' but 'Do we worship a God who is worthy of our suffering?'

So much of our thinking is self-centred. As Dr Dunn points out, the major theme of the book of Job is not 'Why do Christians suffer?' but 'Why do men serve God?' If God were to strip us of everything would we still love and worship him? If we can do so, like Job, we are giving the lie to the devil and we are glorifying God.

3. The only ultimate solution is to cultivate nearness to God

Far more important than any explanation for our suffering is nearness to God in our experience: 'I had a million questions to ask God; but when I met him they all fled my mind and it didn't seem to matter' (Christopher Morley). This is the only way to get things into perspective. That is what happened to Asaph. As he saw the wicked prosper and experienced the chastening of the Lord the whole thing was too painful for him until he went into the sanctuary of God. He came into the presence of God. He listened to God's Word. 'Then' he says 'I understood their end' (*Psa.* 73: 17). He did not just feel good. He had an understanding.

Thomas Boston speaks of communion with God in providence. It is the Word that interprets providence. Providence is the outworking of the will of God in my life. It is because the psalmist was out of fellowship with God that he was in the condition he was in. He had things out of perspective. 'I was as a beast before thee'. When things were back in perspective he could say, 'It is good for me to draw near to God.'

Our responsibility whatever our circumstances is to keep on in the path of duty:

> *Put thou thy trust in God*
> *In duty's path go on.*

People are usually more anxious to get rid of the problem than they are to find the purpose of God in it. 'Afflictions', says Matthew Henry 'are continued no longer than till they have done their work'. It is also our responsibility to pray that our afflictions will be sanctified to us. In his book *Why Us?* Warren Wiersbe speaks of a friend who found herself in a sea of troubles. Attempting to encourage her one day he said 'I want you to know that we are praying for you'. 'I appreciate that', she replied, 'What are you praying God to do?' Wiersbe found himself struggling for an answer and mentioned some things. 'Thank you', she said, 'but please pray for one more request. Pray that I won't waste all this suffering'.

4. We can be assured that the outcome will be 'big with mercy'

'Every work of Christ towards his people', said Ralph Erskine, 'carries something more great and precious in the bosom of it than we are capable at the time of understanding.' William Cowper says something similar in the well-known words

> *Ye fearful saints, fresh courage take;*
> *The clouds ye so much dread*
> *Are big with mercy, and shall break*
> *In blessings on your head.*
>
> *His purposes will ripen fast,*
> *Unfolding every hour;*
> *The bud may have a bitter taste,*
> *But sweet will be the flower.*

We see this frequently in the lives of God's saints. Think of Joseph and his long night of suffering. What a contrast between the prison and the palace! 'They hurt his feet with fetters. He was laid in irons. Until the time that his word came to pass, the word of the Lord tested him'. And then the deliverance: 'The king sent and released him. The ruler of the people let him go free. He made him lord of his house, and ruler of all his possessions, to bind his princes at his pleasure, and teach his elders wisdom' (*Psa.* 105:18–22). It is the timing of providence that is often so wonderful. It is the seasonableness of a mercy that gives such value to it. The engine of God's providence can bring in such a train of happy consequences.

We may not be able to understand our present condition or sufferings because God's providence works on a grand scale. Job had no idea that he was the focus of a battle between God and Satan. God was, as it were, showing off a trophy of his grace. Job thought that his life was useless. At the very moment when he thought all was lost he was doing the greatest thing of all—he was glorifying God, he was giving the lie to the devil. It was twenty-two years after he was thrown into the pit that Joseph discovered the reason why.

Thomas Boston was not able to understand the purpose behind his 'sea of troubles' in Ettrick. He was daily exercised about God's providential dealings. It is there on almost every page of his *Memoirs.* Many would conclude that he was prone to morbid introspection. Whatever tendency to melancholy he may have had he was above all a deeply-exercised saint. The load of suffering he endured has surely an explanation in the abundant fruit that has come from his labours. While men who occupied prominent positions in the Church in his day are largely forgotten the *Works of Boston* are read all over the world.

Our lives resemble the making of a tapestry. The back of it seems to be a mass of tangled and purposeless threads while on the front a beautiful picture is taking shape.

> *Not till the loom is silent*
> *And the shuttles cease to fly*
> *Shall God unroll the canvas*
> *And explain the reason why.*

The dark threads are as needful
In the weaver's skilful hand
As the threads of gold and silver
In the pattern he has planned.

We must look to the end of everything. 'Indeed we count them blessed who endure. You have heard of the patience of Job and seen the end intended by the Lord—that the Lord is very compassionate and merciful' (*James* 5:11).

Conclusion

God has forged an inseparable link between sufferings and glory. That was the road that Christ took. He was made complete as our Saviour 'through sufferings'. He endured. He was without sin.

How much more is suffering part of the road that leads sinners to perfection and glory! What abundant cause we have to be reconciled to our sufferings! 'I always feel much need of God's afflicting hand', wrote Robert Murray M'Cheyne. Said Rutherford: 'Praise God for the hammer, the file and the furnace' and, in similar vein, C. H. Spurgeon wrote, 'This is the place of the furnace, the forge and the hammer'.

We must not be deceived by the current view that invites us to get rid of our troubles and sicknesses and then rejoice. The New Testament calls on us to rejoice *in the midst of sufferings*. Indeed we ought to be alarmed if we have no experience of suffering, for we suffer with him that we may be glorified *together*. There is no glory without suffering.

Sinclair Ferguson in his work *Add to your Faith* recalls seeing a poster on the notice-board of a church which read

WORKSHOP — INSIDE
SHOWROOM — UPSTAIRS

Our lives on earth resemble the workshop. We are in the place of preparation. My life has the chisel of God upon it. Our English word 'character' comes from a Greek word which means an engraving tool, a die for stamping an image. The trials of life can be God's tool for engraving the image of his Son on our character. The experiences may not be enjoyable but they are profitable. Upstairs in the glory God will display the finished articles. They will be like his Son.

God's people never sacrifice or suffer in vain. Our present suffering is an investment in future glory. The sufferings of this present time are not worthy to be compared with the glory. 'How soon you will find', says M'Cheyne again, 'that everything in your history, except sin, has been for you. Every wave of trouble has been wafting you to the sunny shores of a sinless eternity' .

> *Deep waters cross'd life's pathway;*
> *The hedge of thorns was sharp;*
> *Now these lie all behind me;*
> *Oh! for a well-tuned harp!*
>
> *Soon shall the cup of blessing*
> *Wash down earth's bitterest woes;*
> *Soon shall the desert brier*
> *Break into Eden's rose.*

Bibliography

John Flavel	*The Mystery of Providence* (Banner of Truth)
Thomas Boston	*The Crook in the Lot* (Silver Trumpet Publications Ltd)
Samuel Rutherford	*Letters of Samuel Rutherford* (Banner of Truth)
D. M. Lloyd-Jones	*Faith Tried and Triumphant* (IVP)
Warren Wiersbe	*Why Us?* (IVP)
Edith Schaeffer	*Affliction* (Hodder)
Thomas Watson	*All Things for Good* (Banner of Truth)
Murdoch Campbell	*In All Their Afflictions* (Gospel Standard Publications)

Also published by The Banner of Truth Trust

THE MYSTERY OF PROVIDENCE
John Flavel

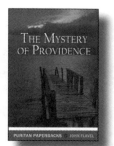

Do we believe that everything in the world and in our own lives down to the minutest details is ordered by the providence of God? Do we ever take time to observe and meditate on the workings of providence? If not, are we missing much?

It should be a delight and pleasure to us to discern how God works all things in the world for his own glory and his people's good. But it should be an even greater pleasure to observe the particular designs of providence in our own lives. 'O what a world of rarities', says John Flavel, 'are to be found in providence . . . With what profound wisdom, infinite tenderness and incessant vigilance it has managed all that concerns us from first to last'.

It was to persuade Christians of the excellency of observing and meditating upon this that Flavel first published his *Mystery of Providence* in 1678. Since then the work has gone through many editions. Based on the words 'God that performeth all things for me' (*Psa.* 57:2) this work shows us how providence works for us in every stage and experience of our lives. The book is richly illustrated from the lives of believers and from the author's wide reading in church history. There are avenues of spiritual knowledge and experience open to the Christian in this work which he probably never new existed.

ISBN 978 0 85151 104 7   224pp.   *paperback*

For details of other helpful publications please contact
THE BANNER OF TRUTH TRUST

3 Murrayfield Road, P O Box 621, Carlisle,
Edinburgh EH12 6EL   PA 17013,
UK   USA

www.banneroftruth.co.uk

Other Booklets in this Series